D0114243

Presented to my friend

Pat,

It is wonderful to have you
as a friend and a "sister"
and to know that it will
be that way for eternally

With love from

In Christ,

Ginny

Because We're Friends

100 Things I Love About You

by
WILLIAM and PATRICIA COLEMAN

VINE
BOOKS
SERVANT PUBLICATIONS
ANN ARBOR, MICHIGAN

Published by Servant Publications, P.O. Box 8617, Ann Arbor, Michigan 48107

Cover design and illustration: PAZ Design Group, Salem, OR
Interior photographs: Bob Foran, Ann Arbor, MI

Printed in the United States of America
ISBN 1-56955-038-7

To

J.C.W.
and a thousand breakfasts

"*A mirror reflects a man's face,
but what he is really like is shown
by the kind of friends he chooses.*"

PROVERBS 27:19, TLB

CONTENTS

Part Five:

Part Six:

"What is the secret of your life?
Tell me, that I may make mine beautiful, too."

He replied:
"I had a friend."

CHARLES KINGSLEY

Just between us. . .

Friendship is a rare treasure that must be used correctly if it is to maintain its value.

Storing it in an attic, protected in a chest under layers of old quilts, will only weaken its condition. Eventually moths will creep in and eat away at the fiber.

Overly used, friendship wears thin and loses its fine texture. Cracks form and edges become frayed. But friendship handled with care and respect will endure and maintain its rich quality. Those are the relationships that both God and humans prize.

This book has been written to help find that good balance.

Bill and Pat Coleman

The Essentials
of Friendship

"Two are better than one, because they have a good return for their work: If one falls down, his friend can help him up. But pity the man who falls and has no one to help him up!... Though one may be overpowered, two can defend themselves. A cord of three strands is not quickly broken."

ECCLESIASTES 4:9-12

Because We're Friends

"Friendship is the greatest of worldy goods.
Certainly to me it is the chief happiness of life."

C. S. LEWIS

O ur friendship isn't just a convenience. We don't get together just to kill time, or only when I need an excuse to get out of the house. Our relationship makes my life sparkle.

Because we're friends
the clouds are never
quite as ominous.

If other parts of my life begin to storm over, I know they can't consume me. The winds can shake me. The rains can sweep over and drench me. But then we get together again to laugh and joke, to share our hopes and disappointments. I walk away a more cheerful person. And the skies clear.

Because we're friends
I feel confident that there is someone who thinks I am worth knowing.

Someone who owes me nothing, and who asks for little but my friendship. Someone who goes out of the way to make me feel wanted. It's the small contacts that make our friendship work. It's the once-in-awhile. The short conversations. Sharing a cup of coffee at a familiar place. Those are the things that make me feel complete.

Because we're friends
I face life's challenges straight on.

You make me feel like I can win. You also make me feel like if I lose, that's all right, too. I can face each bend in the road, each dip along the highway. If I crash, your presence helps me to pull myself out of the wreckage. Win or lose, up or down, I give you a call. No matter how it's going, you hang in there and stay steady as a mountain.

Because we're friends
the sun always shines someplace.

And when we get together I feel rays of warm companionship reaching through you into my life.

A Good Friend…

Accepts tomatoes from your garden
            and quietly gives them away.

Takes a kitten home
            from Fluffy's second litter.

Gives you a couple of dollars
            for your walk against hunger.

Samples your fifth grader's
            home economics cooking project.

Does not see the crooked line
            on the wallpaper in the hall.

Never adds an addendum
            to your long, long list of guilt.

Lets your kids tie him up
            to play "frontiersman."

Leaves the last chocolate caramel in the box for you—
            and eats the pink mint.

"A friend doesn't go on a diet because you are fat. A friend never defends a husband who gets his wife an electric skillet for her birthday. A friend will tell you she saw your old boyfriend—and he's a priest."

ERMA BOMBECK

Friends Know What to Say

"Most people will tell you what loyal friends they are, but are they telling the truth?"
PROVERBS 20:6, TLB

How can you tell if someone is a special friend? Not a casual, once-in-awhile, on-the-fringe kind, but someone who really understands you? Listen to how she talks. Good friends always know what to say. And you are a very special friend.

Good friends **forgive your human quirks.**

Like the time you told me chocolate is actually a health food and essential to your mental well-being. Or the time you reassured me that you often overcook the nacho dip just the way I did.

Good friends
applaud your weakest efforts to improve yourself.

They say you look like you've lost two pounds when the fact is you've gained three. When you can't afford a new coat, a good friend will tell you the wide lapel coat you are wearing is coming back in style.

Good friends
appreciate your "hidden talents."

A special friend tells you your voice has an unusual quality and that you should sing more (but not necessarily where you should sing more). A good friend listens as you read a poem you wrote, then smiles and says you have a gift.

Good friends
are quick to forgive.

When your child breaks the candy dish, a real friend says it was his fault for not putting the dish away. Good friends never lie, but they can be quite creative with the way they phrase things.

Thanks for being such a good friend.

"A friend is a person with whom I may be sincere. Before him, I may think aloud."
RALPH WALDO EMERSON

Friends Don't Try to Change Each Other

"I am the Lord—I do not change.
That is why you are not already utterly
destroyed [for my mercy endures forever]."
MALACHI 3:6, TLB

When Wendy gave up her job at the bank, her parents were stunned. How could she? Wendy's parents weren't sheepish about giving their opinions.

What did she think she was doing, giving up her promising career? And to do what? To work at a local dinner theater—acting, directing, painting sets, looking for part-time work when the seasons were slow. No benefits. Minimal pay. Their daughter, the starving artist. Is that how a young lady should be thinking?

Wendy's boss at the bank suggested she seek counseling before making a final decision. Her brother tried to reason with her. Even the lady at the salon tried to talk her out of it. Everyone wanted Wendy to change her mind.

Everyone except Erin, that is. Erin, her best friend since high school, quietly accepted Wendy's decision. That's the way it had always been. If Wendy wanted a chili dog, Erin ate one, too. If Wendy dated a nerd, Erin said he was OK. Even when Wendy wore that terrible orange thing to the homecoming dance, Erin buttoned her lip.

Erin knew some important secrets about friendship.

Friends don't
try to be parents,
financial advisers,
or fashion police.

Friends don't

manipulate, control, or force their opinions on those they care about. Friends don't try to make others fit their own preconceived mold.

We like our friends because of who they are ... not because we want to change them. Let them be butchers, bakers, or candlestick makers. Let them give up seniority, tenure, and security. But most of all, let them be themselves.

Friends don't

try to change each other.

A Safe Place to Be

"Your best friend is the person who brings out the best that is within you."
HENRY FORD

Friends can disagree. Everybody knows that. Democrats and Republicans can hang out together. Classical and country music fans have been known to share a pot of coffee, or sit side by side in church.

Seldom are friendships based on total agreement. The healthy ones are free to see life from different angles. Different experiences. Different dreams.

What really draws two people together and holds them there is a feeling that each person is safe in the presence of the other.

Friends can talk, speculate, and say what they think. And they know they will be heard, appreciated, and even understood. That's what happens in safe places. We can be ourselves and feel accepted.

A friend can
hear us say something really dumb and not treat us like we're really dumb.

A friend is someone who never embarrasses or ridicules us when we make mistakes. A friend often lets me choose the video we watch—even if my last pick was terrible.

Life now and then gets much harsher than it ought to be. Motorists beep their horns, shout obscenities, and make insulting hand gestures. The new boss at work doesn't care if we live or die. Even the dog seems ungrateful.

But there is a place. There is a person who will take us in, give us a cup of coffee, and be excited to see us again.

Robins have nests.
Bears have caves.
Foxes have holes.
People have friends.

The Code of Caring

"A person who loves innocent thoughts and kind words will have even the king as a friend."
PROVERBS 22:11, NCV

True friends have an unwritten code. They know in their hearts what they will do and what they won't. They try to help, never hurt, the ones they care for.

Even the best of us forget once in awhile what the code says. So let's write it down. A code of caring friendship begins with a few basic principles.

Good friends protect.
They do not spread rumors or gossip.

Good friends support.
They can be counted on in
good times and bad.

Good friends are flexible.
They know how to give and take,
and do not always demand their own way.

Good friends have a short memory
(to forget the bad things)
and a long memory
(to remember the good).
The best friends use the right kind
of memory in every situation.

Good friends are honest.
They "speak the truth in love"
(Ephesians 4:15).

Good friends listen.
When there is a need, they make
time even when it isn't convenient.

Good friends are discreet.
They are careful with secrets. You never
hear through the grapevine what two
friends have spoken in confidence.

Good friends have integrity.
They never agree to do
something they know is wrong,
and never ask someone to do something
they wouldn't do themselves.

Good friends do not impose.
They know when it's OK to ask for
favors—and when it's better not to.

Good friends are generous.
They go the extra mile.
Then they go one mile more.

Other "rules of friendship" between two people can change over the course of time, and sometimes even alter the nature of that relationship.

Good friends are flexible
enough to make those changes, and faithful enough never to compromise on the essentials.

Unstudied Friendship

"A righteous man is cautious in friendship,
but the way of the wicked leads them astray."
PROVERBS 12:26

These days there are studies done on every subject under the sun. What are the effects of being a middle child? Are girls more expressive than boys? How do field mice select their mates? And so the studies go.

Naturally there are studies about friendship: Is it true that two-thirds of friendships are actually power struggles designed to give one person the advantage over the other? I don't know. I don't care.

I don't want to hear about supportive friendships, contrasting friendships, fringe friendships, core friendships, and even sporadic friendships.

Forgive me if I don't care to become a lab rat in scientific research. Some things are better left unstudied.

Could a botanist improve the scent or the beauty of a rose through long, extended research? No. Hybrid roses, while beautiful, have not a fraction of the aroma of those found in a country garden.

Our friendship is like a rose.
It is beautiful, full of life …
but suffers under too much scrutiny
and analysis.

When you listen intently and warmly to a story that means so much to me, I don't have to call a behavioral scientist to find out what that means.

You and I connect,
**and I am all the more fulfilled
because of that connection.**

It doesn't take a survey or a genetic experiment to tell me how real this is.

Let me make a promise. I will accept our friendship on its face value. I won't look for hidden meanings. Let's allow our friendship to unfold, and accept it as it comes. I don't know what it means, but I certainly know how much.

A Friend's Faults

*"Love keeps no record of wrongs....
It always protects, always trusts,
always hopes, always perseveres."*
1 CORINTHIANS 13:5B, 7

The other day I sat by the window and took pen in hand to write down my friend's faults. I thought it would be good to admit to myself his ugly warts, glaring errors, and more than a few flaws. Good friends, I told myself, can accept each other's weaknesses as well as their strengths.

For some time I tried to recall the rude remarks, the broken promises, the lack of consideration. But each time an incident came to mind the memory quickly turned and ran away. It was like trying to grab a cloud of smoke with bare hands, each dark puff faded through my fingers.

At last I put the paper down. I lay the pen beside it.

I'm sure you must
have your faults.
But I prefer to remain in the sunshine of your most obvious gifts.

And I don't need a pen to record those.

Friends Don't Always Agree

"Animals are such agreeable friends—
they ask no questions, they pass no criticisms."
GEORGE ELIOT

Friends don't always have to agree with us. Sometimes we don't even agree with ourselves. It's too much to expect another person to always shake his head "Yes," to nod and go along.

Thanks
for not agreeing all the time.
Disagreements are one of
the important ways I grow.

Nor do we need friends who feel they have to disagree all the time. We become worn out being around someone who fights everything we say, who knows the exception to every rule, who likes to argue for the sake of arguing.

After awhile it's too painful to talk to someone who nit-picks every comment. We begin to speak less and less around people who argue more and more. On the other hand, it isn't very satisfying to be around people who agree all the time. Both kinds of friendships are predictable and boring.

In the long run,
**the friends who tend to count most
are the ones who merely
try to understand.**

They don't have to like our music, but they try to understand why we like it. They don't have to agree with our politics, but neither do they belittle them. They don't have to like the same movies, but sometimes they go along anyway.

Good friends
want to know what makes our hearts slow down, speed up, or even skip a beat.

Friends don't always agree. But understanding is far more valuable than agreement. Understanding will keep shining long after arguing fades away.

Lord, instead of a hundred friends who agree with me, give me one friend who is willing to merely understand what my heart is like.

Friendship at Any Price?

"Do not make friends with a hot-tempered man, do not associate with one easily angered."
PROVERBS 22:24

I'm glad we didn't meet in a frenzied search for friendship. We weren't desperate to attach to someone. We came together comfortably, then saw how much we enjoyed each other's company.

Our friendship
is healthy, even robust.
Its vitality makes me feel
for people who are not as blessed.

Have you ever wondered what would induce someone to join a gang or stay in an abusive relationship? One teenage girl told us that she hung out with "bad people," people "on the edge," because she didn't click with "good people." When she had tried in the past they made fun of her, ridiculed her appearance, and talked disparagingly about her family.

She said that the high-risk types accepted her as she was and cared about her. If she had a problem, they came through. Their acts of "caring" blinded her to what others saw. She saw them as the truly good people.

But were they good for her?

Good people do not abuse their friends.

Good people do not cheat or lie to friends.

Good people do not ask friends to lie or cheat.

Good people do not ask friends to break the law.

Good people do not put their friends at risk.

"Love each other as much as I love you.
And here is how to measure it—
the greatest love is shown when a person
lays down his life for his friends;
and you are my friends if you obey me."

JOHN 15:12-14, TLB

A Pledge of Friendship

"We cannot tell the precise moment when friendship is formed. As in filling a vessel drop by drop, there is at last a drop which makes it run over; so in a series of kindnesses, there is at last one which makes the heart run over."

JAMES BOSWELL

There was no way to give Felicia anything. She was so particular that no one could please her. A vase, a scarf, a beautiful bouquet, a bracelet; no matter what the gift, she turned them all down.

She liked feeling self-sufficient.

She knew what she wanted and could get it herself.

She never wanted to feel beholden to anyone.

It was tough being Felicia's friend. She had never learned the humble act of receiving.

People like Felicia make me think of the apostle Peter. He wanted to wash other people's feet, but would allow no one to touch his own. And Jesus told him he had the wrong idea.

If we give favors to our friends but refuse to accept them, we do not have an equal friendship. Givers and takers must take turns, or the relationship gets out of balance. We must always try to help the needy, the less fortunate, the less clever. But there are times when we need to let others express their love for us when we are the needy and less fortunate. That, too, is a gift.

The person who gives
**but refuses to receive
knows little about gift-giving,
and even less about companionship.**

It is the give and take of friendship that turns the wheel of life.

From this day forth let us make a pledge: When one of us extends his hand with help or gifts or generosity, the other will smile from ear to ear and gratefully accept.

The Best Times
Are Those
We Share Together

"Oh, the comfort, the inexpressible comfort of feeling safe with a person, having neither to weigh thoughts nor measure words, but pouring them all out, just as they are, chaff and grain together, certain that a faithful hand will take and sift them, keep what is worth keeping, and then with the breath of kindness blow the rest away."

DINAH MARIA MULOCK CRAIK

Friendship:
The Icing on the Cake of Life

"Friendship is the source of the greatest pleasures, and without friends even the most agreeable pursuits become tedious."
THOMAS AQUINAS

Tomorrow morning, around ten o'clock, a friend will look another friend in the eye and slowly bite into a donut. Between sips of coffee he will begin to describe in great detail how pin number seven shivered, wiggled, paused, and finally fell dead on the floor in lane fourteen.

Friendship isn't about extraordinary tales. Rare indeed are the times I do anything especially heroic, like pulling a toddler from a well or rescuing a wide-eyed cat off a shaking limb. The stories we share are often typical and mundane.

But that's one of the things I love about our friendship.

Even these everyday stories
become both special and exciting when we share them.

My fish doesn't have to be extra long, or the mountain especially high. I don't have to exaggerate the evening colors stretching across a southwestern desert.

The simple truth
itself is enough to capture your genuine interest.

Of course, it works both ways. A walk through a city park becomes a trek through the wilderness when you paint the scene.

Who could ever count the number of pins that have crashed against the walls in bowling alleys throughout this land? Surely a million or more tumble, smash, and dance around every night of the week. They cause little note, nor are they long remembered. On the other hand ...

Sharing with a friend
**can turn anything into
a magical moment.**

Remember?

"If I had to give a piece of advice to a young man about a place to live, I think I should say, 'Sacrifice almost everything to live where you can be near your friends.' I know I am very fortunate in that respect."

C.S. LEWIS

I'll never forget the day we first became friends. I had ninety cents, you had sixty-three, and we were both really thirsty. So we pooled our resources and bought soft drinks at the old drug store.

Our friendship is full
of priceless memories like these, special moments that form a lasting bond.

Some involve an ordinary kind of fun. Like the time we put on your father's warm clothes and watched the Oklahoma football game in the middle of an ice storm.

Other memories are nice, too. Like sitting on lawn chairs in the shade at an all day gospel sing. Grilling steaks with our spouses at the state park. Playing cards and laughing until dawn at New Year's Eve parties.

Some memories are bittersweet. I remember the day after your surgery when I made you laugh and pull your stitches. And I'll never forget the terrible night someone called and said your airplane was missing. Long, lonely hours passed before a call came back ... it was all a misunderstanding.

Still others are hilarious, at least in retrospect. Like the day you sank up to your hips in the soft sand in the river bed and I had to pull you out. Or the time we got stuck in snow and had to push my car halfway home.

There are other, more significant milestones as well. Your daughter's wedding. My father's funeral. Each event broadened the foundation of our lifelong friendship.

Each memory is more memorable simply because we share it.

I Saw a Show Last Night

*"Grief can take care of itself,
but to get the full value of joy
you must have somebody to divide it with."*
MARK TWAIN

Walking through the park with a longtime friend, Ted aimlessly kicked at a stone and said, "I saw this show on television last night..."

Fortunately, Frank had seen the same program. It was one of those history programs, an old film of Russian troops charging in on horseback, tanks scuttling across the terrain. A mysterious train, probably the one carrying Lenin, could be seen slowly passing in the distance. The revolution was on.

Frank and Ted enjoyed the details of battle and intrigue. At the time, Ted had been tempted to call Frank and tell him the show was on, then decided the hour was too late.

The funny thing was, Ted never considered asking his wife to watch with him. It wasn't the kind of program Ted's wife found fascinating. But that was OK. A friendship forged by marriage has its own special shows to watch. So Ted thought to himself, "I've got to tell Frank about this tomorrow."

Intently he watched the details, noted the expressions, listened carefully for the exact wording. The program came alive for Ted because he had a friend who would be eager to hear about it. Our friendship is like that, too....

Because we're friends,
we can share our common interests,
and learn to appreciate new ones.
By sharing, we both get a taste
of life's finest flavors.

A Chocolate Friendship

"Ah, how good it feels!
The hand of an old friend."
HENRY WADSWORTH LONGFELLOW

The great thing about eating chocolate is that we don't have to. Vegetables, dairy products, fruits, and breads may be essential in our diet, but chocolate is not. When I pick up a bar of chocolate candy, it's a voluntary act. A delicious, comforting, energizing voluntary act.

That's what I like about our friendship. My life could go on without seeing you, but it wouldn't have the same satisfying flavor.

People who work together have a peculiar relationship. Workers report to the same place automatically, whether they like it or not. The clock hits a magic number, and half a dozen people appear in the same room.

Generally they get along fine. The majority are good enough people. But despite all they have to offer, these are forced friendships. Coworkers have to find a way to get along. They need to pull in the same direction, smile at each other, and adapt to idiosyncrasies. Sometimes they avoid each other.

But it's not that way with us. Friends don't sit by the phone thinking, "Oh, rats, I ought to call." If we feel trapped, the friendship is in serious trouble.

I don't have to call you.
The thing is, I want to.

When the phone rings I never say to myself, "Oh, I hope that isn't my friend again." Instead, my pulse quickens with excitement. I hope it is you.

Chocolate candy makes me hungry. Even a picture of chocolate makes my taste buds perk up. Thankfully, the thought of spending an afternoon with you makes me feel the same way— and it's a lot less fattening!

Looking Through an Old Shoebox

I've never been much of a scrapbook person. Something about putting stuff in order and pasting it down in straight lines puts me off. But sometimes, more by accident than design, I find myself sitting by an old open box. And when I do, I can't resist picking up a slip of paper here, focusing on a photo there.

Times like this remind me how close we've been.

I reach into the box and draw out a picture of the two of us at Hanover Park. There we are, the two of us holding up one scrawny fish. Smiling like we had just survived two weeks in the outback.

I put my hand in the box again. The postcard you sent me when you spent a week on the coast. I remember my heart filling up because you took time to write your old buddy. With a million things to do, still you dropped me a note. It meant a lot.

Next, out comes an old tassel from graduation. The red is faded but I can remember when the color was bright. I remember how it hung down over your smiling face. I bet you have yours buried away somewhere, too.

Do you still have the program of our school play when we were juniors? You were one of the leads; it made everyone so proud. I think I was a tree or a phone booth or some dumb thing like that. It seems silly spending time looking in an old box. But these are memories that make me feel good.

I reach my hand one more time into the box. It's a picture of your first child. He's got your smile. Somehow I never thought of you being a parent. Parenting sounds so old. It includes responsibility and maturing and all those things I thought you and I would always avoid.

I close the lid on the box. Enough. I've got things to do. But I'm glad I took a minute to remember you, remember how much our friendship has meant to me. I realize today, more than ever, how much we had.

Keep that smile on your face.
And every once in a while, don't forget to go through your old shoeboxes.

Friendship's
Silver Lining

*"When three of Job's friends heard of all the
tragedy that had befallen him,
they got in touch with each other and traveled from
their homes to comfort and console him....
They sat upon the ground with him silently for seven
days and nights, no one speaking a word;
for they saw his suffering was too great for words. "*

JOB 2:11, 13, TLB

Let Me Help

"Pride goes before destruction
and haughtiness before a fall."
PROVERBS 16:18, TLB

Let's face it. You can be a tad too indepen-dent, a bit of a perfectionist. (But don't change a thing. The last thing a real friend wants to do is to change the other person into some-thing she isn't.)

I enjoy you because of
who you are, not for who
you might some day become.

I do have one request. Would you please open up a little more and let me help? I don't want to intrude. It's just that sometimes I think I could lift your burden an inch or two if you would only let me.

Do you need a quart of milk? Let me stop by the store and pick it up for you. I'm going near there anyway. A dozen cookies for a PTA meeting? Why not let me bake them for you?

I find a great deal of pleasure **in being helpful to you once in awhile.**

So the next time you want someone to hold the ladder, pick up the laundry, or feed the cats, don't forget to let me help.

Therapeutic Friendships

*"Share each other's troubles and problems,
and so obey our Lord's command."*
GALATIANS 6:2, TLB

Cindy is not a counselor. And if someone should ask her what to do about depression or insomnia, Ellen wouldn't have a clue.

But once a week the two of them get together and walk in the mall. Sometimes they purchase an item, but usually they don't. They stop for a cup of coffee, and sometimes munchies. And as their coffee cools, they pray for the things that most concern them.

They talk about many things. Cindy never tries to play shrink. Ellen never tries to "parent" Cindy with lists of shoulds and oughts. They simply enjoy being together, sharing and praying with each other. They find it the best kind of therapy. Each outing makes them feel less anxious and stronger to face the day.

Their time together energizes them. Talking and listening, laughing at styles and prices gives them balance. Cindy doesn't try to fathom the depths of Ellen's psyche. Ellen doesn't try to pinpoint the source of Cindy's angst.

Their friendship,
like ours, doesn't solve all problems,
but because of it
the problems never get
too big to handle.

Grown-Up Friends

"There are 'friends' who pretend to be friends, but there is a friend who sticks closer than a brother."
PROVERBS 18:24, TLB

In the fifth grade I worried a great deal about friends. I wanted to know if anyone liked me, and worried about being excluded. Almost daily I looked for a sign that I was "in," that I was popular, one of the gang. Like a flying goose, I didn't want to be left out of the big "V" moving across the sky of life.

Being left off a party list was the worst. Who got invited to whose birthday was the most important news in the world. Sometimes I would count the parties I was not invited to.

That was the fifth grade.

It's a lot different now. I'm a long way from grade school parties, junior high dances, and high school car rides out into the country. I'd like to think I'm also miles away from hoping people will "be my friend."

Still, I have to admit that occasionally I still wonder who likes me. But somewhere in my slowly maturing soul I've learned it is just as important to be a friend as it is to have a friend.

Today I want to be your friend.
I want to listen to what you have to say.
I want to hear about your children,
your car, and your in-laws,
your dreams and hopes.

I'd like to share my thoughts with you, too; but that isn't my main purpose.

Fifth-graders are often too overwhelmed with their own rapidly changing lives to listen to someone else's heart. But at my age I should have broad enough shoulders to hold up someone else's burden now and then. And if my acts of thoughtfulness make it easier for you to be my friend, then I am twice blessed.

"Friends are an aid to the young,
To guard them from error;

"To the elderly,
To attend to their wants and to
supplement their failing power of action;

"To those in the prime of life,
To assist them to noble deeds."

ARISTOTLE

When Things Go Wrong

"Real friendship is shown in times of trouble;
Prosperity is full of friends."
EURIPIDES

Sometimes relationships go haywire. We get sloppy, and say or do things we shouldn't. We forget the difference between being frank and being ugly. But good friends like you understand the occasional slipup.

You overlook it
when once in a blue moon I cross the boundaries of kinship.

You forgive my snarls and gripes at the end of a bad day. You just clear your head, shake it off, and stay close.

I have known people who believed that friendship is a license for verbal abuse. They felt friendship gave them the right to make rude comments, harsh criticisms, and "affectionate" insults. These "friendships" never last.

If I say something
that sounds unkind,
please try to forgive me.

If I take you for granted, and sometimes I do, try to be patient. Once in awhile I'm as sensitive as concrete. I don't intend to be thoughtless. We all have lapses. Just don't suffer in silence. Let me know I've hurt you. I don't want to keep doing anything that will bring pain to your life. I need you to gently remind me when I am not being a loving friend.

Let's help each other
live up to the "standard" of love.

Forgive Me

"Love is patient and kind; love is not jealous or boastful; it is not arrogant or rude.
Love does not insist on its own way; it is not irritable or resentful;
it does not rejoice at wrong, but rejoices in the right.
Love bears all things, believes all things, hopes all things, endures all things.
Love never ends."

1 CORINTHIANS 13:4-8a, RSV

It wasn't until I was halfway home that I realized what I had done. In the middle of your conversation, while you were explaining how you felt about something important, I cut in to tell my story. Only later did I comprehend what an insensitive mistake I had made.

I wonder how many times I've pushed aside your feelings just to hear myself talk. I responded to your deepest concerns with little more than a trite phrase or cold shrug.

I'm sorry. Forgive me?

I'm sure my actions have at times left you bewildered. You're too kind to say anything, and so I don't always realize how much my thoughtless words and actions hurt you. I think of all the times you tried to get me to go with you, times you just wanted my company, and I found "something better" to do. Some shallow book taught me that I don't have to do anything I don't want to do, or go anywhere I don't want to go. How callous I can be!

Remind me to toss that old, self-absorbing book away. I need to pick up another guide, one that teaches me how to look after the needs of my friends.

When I forget and pick up the wrong book again, forgive me.

You are my favorite illustration of what true friendship is all about.

Sometimes when I say or do the wrong thing, it's because I don't know what you need, don't know how to respond to your despair. The loss of your job. The death of your father. The long weeks when you wondered whether your marriage would ever float again, let alone sail the waves of wedded bliss. All I really wanted was for you to buck up, to get a grip and act like you were happy.

When your daughter didn't come home all night, I tried to get you to look at the bright side, to think positively. I'm sorry I didn't allow you to express the darkness you were feeling, or try to accept your agony.

Friends hurt with those who are hurting.
They know how to "weep with those who weep."

Forgive me for not being more supportive. I can't guarantee that I will be better in the future. I want you to know I intend to try.

But on those occasions when I hurt you without meaning to, I want to ask you in advance ... forgive me.

"It is one of the blessings of old friends that you can afford to be stupid with them."
RALPH WALDO EMERSON

Making Choices

"I'm afraid to confront him about it." Lisa and Tammy sat on the bench in the mall, soft drinks firmly in hand.

"Have you tried?" Tammy asked with mild concern.

"Jerry comes home later every night," Lisa continued. "Maybe it's my imagination. But I don't think so."

"How long has this been going on?" Tammy propped her package next to the trash container.

"A couple of months. Maybe ten weeks. At first it was thirty minutes to an hour. Then it was past supper. Recently it's been nine or ten o'clock."

"Boy, that is late. Have you mentioned it to him?"

"He just shrugs it off and says work is getting hectic this time of year. He doesn't seem eager to talk. Jerry just buries his head in the paper or flips on the TV."

"What do you think you should do now?" Tammy wondered aloud.

"I don't know. What do you think?"

Tammy hesitated. "It's hard. Sounds like you might need some time alone with him. You could take him to breakfast on Saturday morning. Or how about a walk in the park? You could find a place there to sit together and talk."

"No way I can just let it ride." Lisa looked out across the mall. "But I hate to make it sound too serious."

"But you are worried," Tammy ventured.

"Sure I am."

"Maybe a Chinese dinner would be good. You know, the restaurant you went to when you were dating."

Lisa trusted Tammy to help her with important decisions like this. Of course, Tammy never tried to solve Lisa's problems for her. That was one of the things Lisa liked most about her friend. Tammy would listen. She would even make a few general suggestions. But Tammy never tried to take decision-making away from her friend. She knew an important secret about friendship.

Good friends don't try to "push"
their own solutions to every problem.
Instead they inspire confidence in
the other person's ability to decide.

After talking to Tammy, Lisa felt able to pull herself together and create her own plan. With dignity she could take responsibility and do what she knew had to be done. Her friend didn't shackle her with unwanted advice. Tammy simply laid out a smorgasbord of choices and handed Lisa a plate.

Most of us are willing
to take responsibility
for the choices we make.
But we appreciate someone who will
"set the table" with a few ideas.

The Miracles of Friendship

"A friend loves you all the time."
PROVERBS 17:17A, NCV

It's happened many times. Just last week, when I was feeling blue, you called just to ask for one of my recipes. "Nobody knows their way around a kitchen like you." That comment made me smile for the rest of the day.

You always seem to know
just when I need you.

Is it mere coincidence? I don't think so. I think it's those times when God prompts you to be one of his special messengers.

Sometimes you've called with something important to say, or maybe just to relate a humorous incident.

The reason you call
is of little significance.
But often the timing is simply uncanny.

I know you too well to entertain any thoughts that you might be an angel. I'm glad you're not. Sometimes your earthy nature is all too evident.

But now and again
your touch, your timing,
your presence is truly grace-filled.

Clouds move in on me in the most unlikely seasons sometimes. Even when things should be going well, sometimes a dark shadow covers me and I want to hide in a closet. Just the other day I was getting ready to slink off, pouting, when I heard a knock on the door.

"Someone selling something," I groused as I dragged myself to the door. There you stood.

"Can't stay," you smiled. "I found this book when I was shopping. Thought you might like it." And with that you hustled back to your car. The engine was still running.

I stood there, book in hand. Then a grin spread over my face; it was like my heart got a jump-start.

I know that,
technically, your appearance doesn't qualify as a miracle. Then again, who's to say?

If I had any sense I would stop trying to figure it out. Instead I would simply thank God for you. And I do. Indeed I do.

"Do not keep the alabaster boxes of your love and tenderness sealed up until your friends are dead. Fill their lives with sweetness. Speak approving, cheering words while their ears can hear them, and while their hearts can be thrilled and made happier by them."

GEORGE CHILDS

Friendship
with God

"Greater love has no one than this,
that he lay down his life for his friends."
JOHN 15:13

God Wants to Be Friends with Me

"And so it happened just as the Scriptures say, that Abraham trusted God, and the Lord declared him good in God's sight, and he was even called 'the friend of God.'"
JAMES 2:23, TLB

When I was younger I pictured the face of God having a frown. I had grown up to believe that God had zero sense of humor. In my mind he had a stern forehead, deep wrinkles, and tight lips. The only Heavenly Father I knew as a child seemed angry, disgruntled, and sour.

I understood the fear of God. I understood the power of God. I understood the judgment of God. I even understood the anger of God. I firmly believed that God was sorely disappointed in me. Everything I did was some shade of wrong. I always thought God merely tolerated me.

For a long time I thought God had no friends. I always imagined him in a category all his own, with no room for mere people. No one told me that God wanted to be my friend, just as he was Abraham's friend.

Then someone explained it to me, but I still didn't completely understand. If I called God and said I had tickets to the game Saturday, would he want to go? How would he fit in the car? And would he order a hot dog or pizza?

Now I know the truth. The Lord of the universe does indeed want to go with me wherever I go … to a baseball game, to the mall, or even just when I'm driving into town.

God wants to be with me.
He gets excited about hanging out.
All day, every day. Like a real friend.

It was startling at first to learn that I can know God. Even more amazing to find out that he wants to get to know me, too. Of course, I wasn't always sure if I wanted God around all day long. Now I understand how good a trip that can be.

"May God's love and the Holy Spirit's friendship be yours."
2 CORINTHIANS 13:14B, TLB

Fold Up the Ladder

"I have friends in overalls
whose friendship I would not swap
for the favor of the kings of the world."
THOMAS A. EDISON

I'm hardly the type of person that people try to meet so they can look good.

Not that I'm a bad sort. But no one would think of me and "social register" in the same sentence. Not with my eleven-year-old subcompact car and my Detroit Tigers sweatshirt. My idea of a good time is driving to the sandhills to watch the cranes migrate, not jetting to the Riviera.

I won't judge people who pick friends with the intent of using them as a stairway to the top. To each his own. If playing golf with the socially elite is important to someone, who am I to wish them a double bogey?

Somehow, though,

it feels good to know that
neither of us became friends
in order to use the other.
We can both breathe clear air
on that account.

That's how I picture Christ selecting his friends. He included a tax collector here, a sinner or two there. They weren't necessarily good career choices for him, but the Son of God reached out anyway.

I can imagine Jesus walking through our town. Suddenly he stops, points a finger, and says warmly, "Hey, come over here. Yeah, you with the eleven-year-old car."

It may be a foolish thought, but it makes me feel good.

He Died for His Friends

"Why, one will hardly die for a righteous man— though perhaps for a good man one will dare even to die. But God shows his love for us in that while we were yet sinners Christ died for us."

ROMANS 5:7-8, RSV

The cross is the most convincing sign of God's enduring friendship. If we were to live a hundred years, we could barely begin to understand what it all meant. The eternal war between the forces of good and evil for the souls of humanity was won that day with a decisive victory. And yet, in the midst of that anguish, we do know this: Jesus died for his friends.

It's too much to comprehend sometimes. Even when we were not his friends, God was our Friend. His Son willingly shed his innocent blood, an agony that only he could have fully experienced. Christ gave himself up in an ultimate act of love and caring.

How could he have loved billions of people he had never seen, people who would not be born for thousands of years? Such truth boggles the mind. And yet, in the midst of that anguish we do know this: Jesus died for his friends.

One by one, person by person, Jesus Christ died for us, his friends.

The cross shows us that God can act in friendship toward those who do not consider themselves his friends.

We must follow his example
**and extend acts of friendship
to those who are not yet our friends.**

Not Servants, but Friends

" I no longer call you servants, because a servant does not know his master's business. Instead, I have called you friends. "

JOHN 15:15A

Two thousand years ago, a change occurred that continues to affect our lives today. This change was far more profound and far-reaching than any discovery or invention before or since— more important than penicillin, the airplane, or even atomic energy!

What change was that? Two thousand years ago, Jesus Christ told his followers that from then on he would no longer call them servants. From that day and forever he would call them friends.

Imagine his followers' reactions as they listened in amazement to those words. Maybe they inched closer to be sure they had heard correctly.

One disciple might have cleared his ear with one finger. Another could have pinched himself to see if he were dreaming.

Why would God incarnate want to share his intimate thoughts and plans with such earth-bound, flaky sinners? No one knows. But from that moment on, life was never the same for these men.

"I call you friends," Jesus said. He has extended that same invitation to us today. And he never withdraws that intimacy from anyone who follows him. We never walk alone. He is our greatest Friend of all.

"Be thou familiar, but by no means vulgar;
Those friends thou hast, and their adoption tried,
Grapple them to thy soul with hoops of steel."
WILLIAM SHAKESPEARE

Jonathan and David

"Go in peace, for we have sworn friendship with each other in the name of the Lord."

1 SAMUEL 20:42A

Since I was a child, the names David and Jonathan have come to symbolize the essence of true friendship. Of course, there are many reasons why these two men should not have been friends. But the Bible tells us that after David triumphed over Goliath, Jonathan "became one in spirit with David, and he loved him as himself" (1 Samuel 18:1).

Unfortunately Jonathan's father, King Saul, resented David. From the moment the king heard the women singing and cheering in the streets about the great young warrior (see 1 Samuel 18:9), Saul wanted to kill him. The young shepherd was too much of a threat to the king's welfare—and his throne.

How did Jonathan react to this turn of events? Did he side with his father? No, in the midst of family tension and royal fears, Jonathan rose above them. Somehow he knew that the throne belonged not to his own father or even himself, but to his friend.

Every time King Saul tried to kill David, Jonathan intervened. First, he warned David of the danger. Then he persuaded Saul to spare David's life. Ultimately Jonathan brought David and Saul together in an attempt to make peace, but the truce did not hold.

The friendship between these remarkable men, **as with all relationships, must have been strained from time to time.**

Jonathan stood in the gap between his father and his best friend, David, and shielded his friend from his father's rage. Through some of the strangest twists in Biblical history, this friendship remained cemented.

Lord, the story of David and Jonathan
shows us how resilient and steadfast
a good friendship can be.
Help us to always aspire to this ideal.

The Sounds
of Friendship

"In times of emotional struggle, our first recourse
might be to talk with friends, for we know that our
most difficult material is safe with a friend,
and that the friendship can hold our thoughts and
feelings, no matter how painful or unusual,
as we sift through them and watch them unfold."
THOMAS MOORE

Give Me A Call

"A friendly discussion is as stimulating
as the sparks that fly when iron strikes iron."
PROVERBS 27:17, TLB

Even close friends sometimes have trouble calling each other. We think to ourselves: Have I called once too often this week? Am I wearing out my welcome?

Do me a favor. It will mean a lot to me.

If you ever wonder
whether or not to dial my number,
please give me a call.

Call, no matter what the reason.

Maybe you want to go somewhere.

Or maybe you simply want to chat for a few minutes.

Or maybe you've just heard a joke and you're going to split if you don't tell someone.

Give me a call. I enjoy hearing from you. If the time is inconvenient, I promise to tell you to call back later.

If you want to go somewhere or do something, the odds are high that I will want to do it, too. The fact that we can do it together grabs my attention from the start.

When you feel down, frustrated, confused, or hurt, I'd especially like to hear from you. Maybe by listening I can drain a bit of the pain from your brow. That's one of the things friends are for.

I know a phone can be terribly heavy. I hate to think how many times I have picked a receiver up, held it for only a second, and placed it back on the hook, exhausted and frustrated. You must feel that way sometimes, too.

But the next time you stare at the electronic monster, remember this:

There is a reason
**why you know my number
and I know yours.
It's because we have used them so often.**

Pick up the phone. Give me a call.

Storytelling

"**S**he's telling another one of those stories from her childhood," Kim thought to herself. "I've heard before about skating and sledding in northern Minnesota."

Kim was barely listening as Sandy spoke. As Kim sipped coffee, her mind spun with its own plans.

"Maybe when Sandy gets done talking, I can tell her about the time our family got stuck in the snow just south of Cleveland. I like that story. Plus it has a funny ending."

Finally, Sandy wrapped up her story. Kim laughed and said, "That must have been fun. You'd never guess what happened to us in Cleveland. Well, actually it was just south of Cleveland, about thirty miles ..."

It's sad how many times friends do that. Instead of listening to what someone is saying, we are busy trying to think of what we will say. Maybe we want to top the story. Sometimes we're afraid of not having anything to say. Our minds search frantically through our mental attics.

This constant hunt for something to say prohibits us from becoming part of our friend's story.

When two friends share a story,
both the teller and the listener
exchange an important gift.

A story is important to the person who is telling it. A storyteller is presenting a gift, recounting the tale for his friend's enjoyment.

The listener also gives a gift. Time, attention, and caring are presents more valuable than most packages under Christmas trees. Listening is a gift of dignity.

Thanks for listening,
and for being there while I talk.
You are a true friend.

Letting It "All Hang Out"

*"A perverse man stirs up dissension,
and a gossip separates close friends."*
PROVERBS 16:28

"I can't help it," Terri bragged. "I'm just one of those people who has to say what they feel. Sometimes I come across as crude, but that's the way I am."

Mary merely winced and took another sip of coffee. She enjoyed Terri's company, but she didn't appreciate her "let it all hang out" side. She wished her friend would choose certain words more carefully. For that matter, she preferred that Terri wouldn't bring up some subjects at all.

It's one thing to be open and sincere. It's quite another to be tasteless and abrasive. Some things shouldn't "hang out."

Smart friends know
when to zipper up, button down, and tuck some things back inside.

One day a kindly aunt hastily gathered a bushel of apples from her orchard. Her eyesight was not what it used to be, and in the process of collecting the apples she overlooked a few rotten ones, a couple of crushed ones, and a bit of debris.

Working alongside her mother, the old woman's daughter filled another basket with apples. Carefully she chose good apples, discarded the defective ones, and even stopped to polish a few.

Two bushels of apples. The grateful recipient smiled and accepted both baskets, for no one could doubt the sincerity and generosity of the gesture. But one basket was far more beautiful than the other.

Every day we deliver bushels and bushels of words to the people we know best. But once in a while we need to cast out a bad apple, a word or phrase that might hurt, embarrass, offend, or dismay the people we truly care about.

I am thankful for you
because you are careful to give me only the "polished apples" in our basket of friendship.

"Treat your friends as you do your pictures, and place them in their best light."
JENNIE JEROME CHURCHILL

Honest Compliments

*"A word fitly spoken is like apples of gold
in pictures of silver."*
PROVERBS 25:11, KJV

"Your first song was terrific," Becky greeted Angela after the meeting was over. "It almost brought me to tears."

"Oh, thanks!" Angela's face beamed as they quickly hugged. "How did you like the second one?"

"Like I said," Becky smiled again. "I thought the first song was special."

Still locked arm-in-arm, they walked off.

Becky was that kind of friend. She was generous with compliments, but simply refused to flatter. That way her many friends knew she would tell the truth. Uplifting, cheerful, healthy truth.

I'm really lucky.
I have a friend like Becky, too, a friend who makes it a point to encourage me often.

You send honest compliments my way with thoughtful regularity. It lifts my spirits. I've often wondered where you learned how to do this. Maybe a parent or a wise old grandparent taught you. Or maybe you know instinctively that the only compliments that really matter are the ones that are true. Flattery has a sour aftertaste. Insincerity is hard to swallow.

Good friends like you
are important to good mental health. You make me feel better because you see my true potential and help me to see it, too.

Like miners, good friends take the time to seek out the true gems in our lives. They dig around. They get to know us. They sift through the superficial and look for treasures that count.

Thanks for respecting me enough
to offer honest compliments and sincere encouragement.

Thanks for Listening

"I like a highland friend who will stand by me
not only when I am in the right,
but when I am a little in the wrong."
SIR WALTER SCOTT

"Well, actually Pete and I don't have much in common. If I start to think about it, I wonder what keeps us together." Randy, a local store manager, searched to find the right words. "We spend a lot of time together. And the time flies."

What do you talk about?
"Anything that is on our minds. We talk about sports or politics or the news. Whatever we've been reading the past week, or what we've seen on television."

Do you try to solve problems?
"Almost never." A broad smile swept across Randy's face. "Like last week, we spent an hour discussing whether teaching phonics in the

schools was worthwhile. Neither one of us knew what we were talking about, but we kept talking. It didn't solve anything, but we got to air out how we saw things."

Do you argue?
"We disagree. We don't get mad or call each other names. That's not to say I've never gotten mad at Peter, but very seldom. We never get gut-wrenching angry. Most of what we talk about is no big deal."

What's the charm, then? If you don't solve anything, how can you sit for a couple of hours and just talk?
"It isn't the talking so much. I think it's really the listening. When I've read a book or an article, Peter gives me his total attention and listens to what I'm excited about for five or ten minutes, sometimes much more."

Listening means that much to you?
"Of course it does. It isn't the only thing. I'm interested in what Peter has to say. I've gotten a real education over the years just listening to him. Even if he's dead wrong.

"But when he listens, I mean actively asking questions and giving me his full attention, that's a lot of what friendship is to me."

Some people say you can't learn if you are talking.
"Nonsense. I learn a lot by hearing my own voice. I remember it better if I say it out loud. Verbalizing lets me hear how good or silly my view sounds.

"But that's not where it really is. What Peter gives to me is the honor of being a good listener. And I hope that's what I give to him, too."

It isn't so much what we say that binds us as friends. More importantly, it's the fact that we are free to say it.

Words, thoughts, ideas, and feelings can bounce between us in a "safety zone." Every speaker deserves a friend who provides a safe place where he can be heard.

Sharing the Important Things

R eal friends listen closely when you speak
about your faith. Friends don't have to
believe exactly as you do. And it's not a good
idea to "preach." But sometimes our faith over-
flows its banks in a natural way.

That's when it's great to have a friend who listens to our beliefs. Someone who will even hear
our doubts.

One of the reasons
I am thankful for you is that when
the rivers in my heart overflow,
I don't have to hold it in.
You always seem to want to share it with me.

It can be hard to be around people who have
zero "faith tolerance." But friends don't expect
us to restrain ourselves from talking about what is
important to us. We wouldn't think of winning a
cruise trip and keeping it from our friends, or
being cured of cancer and keeping it to ourselves.

Good friends care about the things that matter to us. With casual friends we can talk about clothing and kids. We can get upset at politicians and venture an opinion about the latest diet.

But the deepest kind of friendship allows us to express our faith when it bubbles up inside our hearts.

The Bible tells the story of a man who was possessed by demons. Jesus Christ drove the demons out and let them enter into some hogs. Naturally, the man was tremendously grateful.

"'Go home to your friends,' Jesus told him, 'and tell them what wonderful things God has done for you; and how merciful he has been.'"
MARK 5:19, TLB

Sometimes you just have to tell a friend.

Friends Old and New, *Both* Near and Far

"True is the sentence we are sometimes told;
A friend is worth far more than bags of gold."
LEONORA CHRISTINA

The List

"I have never stopped thanking God for you..."
EPHESIANS 1:16, TLB

I'm not meticulous. I've never been good at keeping lists. But if I listed eight or ten things for which I thank God, you would be high on the list.

Most of all I'm thankful for my family. I'm also grateful for my health. Following that, my heart is filled with gratitude for friends like you.

Way more than the Grand Canyon,
fine dining, or showers of stars,
my heart appreciates your company.

I'm not much of a things person. I'm not strongly attached to gadgets, new electronics, or beautiful vehicles. I can't say that crowds of people mean much to me. But a small pocketful of friends means more to me than rare gems, expensive paintings, or a trip on the Concorde.

If I made the list, it would become simple and plain almost immediately. There near the center I'd write your name. I'd even write your middle name. Can you believe I know your middle name?

I want God to hear about you.
**I want God to know how much
you mean to this soft heart.**

I wouldn't get mushy, though. I'd just tell him what it's like to have such a good friend in my life. And if a tear starts to form, I'll just brush it away.

As I write this letter, it occurs to me that you might not want to know how highly I think of you, how much I care for you. It might make you uncomfortable. If I were smart, maybe I'd throw this letter away and save us both a lot of embarrassment.

It's best not to risk it, I suppose. I won't put your name on a list, after all. I'll just sit here quietly and thank God for what you mean to me, and allow my gratitude to flow out of a sincere heart.

Old Friends

*"Never abandon a friend—either yours or
your father's. Then you won't need to go to a
distant relative for help in your time of need."*
PROVERBS 27:10, TLB

There was a time when our friendship was a
vital part of my life. I was young and overwhelmed, with barely a clue as to which end was
up.

Then you came along
**and helped me through the maze.
I'll never forget that.**

Now we don't see each other any more. The
changes of time and space can pull the best of
friends apart. A thousand miles, a thousand
changing circumstances stand between us. I have
new friends now. But that doesn't mean the
memories of what we shared have gone away.

The memories of our friendship
**are too colorful, too rich,
and too important ever to fade.**

We used to laugh until it hurt, and then we would laugh some more. We told stories: loud, enthusiastic stories until the waitresses gave us stern looks and the host tapped his menu rapidly into the palm of his rigid hand.

*Those everyday moments
of friendship*
**made a lasting impression on me.
So much of who I am today
is because of you.**

We created together. We served together. We "ran around" together. One time we even sat in a lodge by the fire and dried out together after I fell into a frozen lake.

You were always the mature one (but not by much). Older, better educated, and employed.

You were God's shining example in my life.

Of course, when we got together you left half your maturity at home. Thanks for doing that. I needed someone who was very capable—and yet who didn't take life too seriously.

One of the things I most loved about you —you always thought seriousness was far overrated.

When I think of you I picture the disciples walking along the road with Jesus. As they move along they kid each other, pull at each other, and laugh out loud. I learned that years ago from you.

I'll never forget you, old friend.

"I count myself in nothing else so happy As in a soul remembering my good friend."
WILLIAM SHAKESPEARE

The Sidekick

"After this the Lord appointed seventy-two others and sent them two by two ahead of him to every town and place where he was about to go."

LUKE 10:1

The Lord understood the importance of true companionship. As he sent his disciples out to share the good news with the world, he sent them with a partner. Someone to share the load. Not a "sidekick," like in the old western movies—someone to obey, fetch, and follow orders—but a real partner for the journey.

Why is this distinction important? The guy who plays the "sidekick" is never equal to the star; what he has to say is never as important. Even as a kid I knew this; I never wanted to be a sidekick. I didn't have to be the star, but I didn't want to be Mr. Tagalong with the funny-looking horse.

No one wants to be a sidekick. Certainly not in friendship.

Friends don't "trail" one another.
Equality is the only place where a
friendship will grow and thrive.

One of the things
I like best about you
is that we ride together comfortably,
side by side.

*"You cannot be friends upon any other terms
than upon the terms of equality."*
WOODROW WILSON

Sit-Down-and-Listen Friends

"Being friends with Signe isn't like having a sister, because my real sister is mean to me, but it also is like having a sister because we spend so much time together. The best part is when we make jokes about things that happen in school and get silly together."

ANNA FREEDMAN

We were sitting with a group of teenagers one day when our conversation turned to friendship. Immediately we had their full attention. At no other time of life are peers more important or more mystifying than during young adulthood.

And yet when we asked them, "What is a friend?" they all had plenty to say. But there was one answer that gave us a vivid mental picture:

"A friend is someone who will sit down and listen."

Not merely "someone who will listen," but "someone who will *sit down* and listen." What's the difference? Plenty. Consider the alternative: Someone who ...

reads while he listens ...
keeps walking along while he listens ...
looks around the room while he listens ...
keeps interrupting while he listens ...
shifts his weight nervously while he listens ...
counts his change while he listens ...

The true friend is someone who blocks out other distractions. Someone who sits within easy hearing distance. Someone who looks at his friend to see facial expression and body language as well as hear voice tension.

Sometimes well-meaning acquaintances will insist, "You know you can always come and talk to me." And yet they never have time to hear us out.

Thank God for friends like you,
friends of the sit-down-and-listen variety.
I'll try not to wear you out—
I'm just grateful you're there.

A Little Like Marriage

*"Friendship is, of course, another word for love,
love of varying intensity.
The need for friendship, for love, and its main-
tenance, is never-ending."*
ASHLEY MONTAGU

If you have a friend for a long time, the relationship assumes various forms, shapes, and
colors. Friendships are breathing, living, changing encounters. The best friendships are not
unlike marriages with all their attending adventures.

Take our friendship, for example. Our friendship is like a good marriage because ...

We instantly recognize
each other's voice on the telephone.
It always makes the day brighter.

With a glance
I can usually tell if you're serious—
or about to kid me with a tall tale.
(And it works the other way, too.)

At times we may tire
of one another
and wonder if the commitment is worth it.
But we always decide it is.

Sometimes our friendship
seems one-sided,
as though one person is giving
ninety percent of the effort.
But it always evens out.

There are times

when we take each other for granted and are
tempted to sink into common rudeness.
But there are shining moments of sheer
grace when we are there for each other
in ways no one else could be.

When something good happens to one of us,

the other feels the pleasure.
When something bad happens,
the other helps to carry the burden.

We have developed

an ability to anticipate how the other will
react to certain conditions, just as we think
we can predict our spouses' feelings.

For a long time
our relationship might seem
cold and distant—
only to rejuvenate over
the most trivial circumstance.

Our friendship isn't a marriage. Marriage has adventures all its own. And yet, some of the gentle bonds are similar one to the other.

Friends and Spouses

"A true friend is always loyal,
and a brother is born to help in time of need."
PROVERBS 17:17, TLB

Do married people need friends? If you are married, isn't your spouse supposed to be your best friend? Does the fact that you're looking for friends besides your partner mean that your marriage is somehow lacking?

Every relationship needs some relief. Twenty-four-hour friendships create tremendous pressure. That's why we take walks, go shopping, or go to a concert without the person we love the most. It's called space. Every couple needs it.

Neither can we expect our spouse to enjoy everything we like to do. That's the beauty of friendship. The right kind of friend often makes a marriage richer.

A friend
goes with you to your kind of movies.

A friend
explores foreign restaurants
with exotic salad dressings.

A friend
goes with you to gender-specific stores.

A friend
discusses with you the section of the
newspaper that your spouse doesn't read.

A friend
enjoys the endless games of Scrabble
your partner just can't stand.

Friends do all those offbeat, marriage-incompatible things a spouse doesn't enjoy doing. However, a smart friend does not compete with his friend's spouse. If a couple enjoys hikes in the mountains, a smart friend backs off and lets the lovers go their way. Real friends do not steal quality time away from those who are bound at the heart. We tread gently. We know priorities and we respect them.

Spouses and friends. They can be great in tandem. First the marriage. Second the friendship. Placed in order, these important relationships make life run smoothly.

A Friend for
Every Season

"The man who knows right from wrong and has
good judgment and common sense is happier
than the man who is immensely rich!
For such wisdom is far more valuable
than precious jewels."
PROVERBS 3:13-15, TLB

Barb was obviously uncomfortable.

One moment she and Jessica had been having a pleasant personal conversation. The next moment Barb became fidgety and announced that she needed to leave. The children would soon be home, she said, and there were things she had to do. All the while making excuses, she deposited a tip for the waitress and began moving toward the door.

"I'll call you next week." She forced a smile at Jessica as she headed for the exit.

Somewhat bewildered, Jessica wondered why

their discussion had "gone south." Why had Barb reacted so?

But in her heart, she knew the answer.

Whenever Jessica brought up the subject of her husband, Barb reacted the same way. Jessica's marriage was not exactly made in heaven, and sometimes Jessica needed someone to talk to. But Barb never seemed comfortable around the topic of domestic turmoil.

That's all right, Jessica told herself. Different strokes for different folks. She had learned an important lesson in friendship.

Some friends are good for sharing stories. Others are good for going places. Some friends are excellent for discussing faith. Others are better at hands-on, fix-or-paint-it, creative things. Not many friends do all things well.

And a very, very few friends are great at hearing about the pain in our hearts.

I thank God
for the ways you and I "connect."

Farewell to a Friend

*"The Lord watch between me and thee,
when we are absent one from another."*
GENESIS 31:49, KJV

Six years ago, Donna and Anita were the best
of friends. They laughed aloud in restaurants
until people stared. They always went places and
did things together.

But the past three years have seen a slow,
gradual change. No big blowup or deep trauma.
There was no trouble between them. It has been
more like a shift. Inch by inch, the relationship
continues to shift.

Today they seldom call unless there is a specific
reason. Their calls last a couple of minutes and
invariably conclude with, "We need to get together sometime." The other responds, "Boy, it's
been awhile. Say hello to your husband for me."

It has been awhile. And perhaps it would be
good to see each other again. But they aren't
going to. And both of them know it.

Things shifted. Their kids got involved in activities, their jobs changed, and other family needs pressed in on all sides. One morning, sitting in the kitchen all alone, children off to school and husband gone, Donna picked up her coffee cup and held it high.

Thanks for the good times, she thought to herself. For the stories we once told, for the places we have been, for the garage sales we held together, and for the overheated radiator rescue on Route 81.

The good times between them
were a thing of the past.
But the memories are indispensable.

And Donna drank a toast.

If Only for a Season

"One friend in a lifetime is much;

two are many;

three are hardly possible."

HENRY BROOKS ADAMS

What if it turns out that we are to be companions for only a few months or a year? What if one of us needs to move on? What will happen to our friendship if our jobs, educations, or futures call us somewhere else?

That's the chance I'm willing to take.

If our friendship is only for a season, then let it be a full season.

If our sharing is to be counted in weeks and months instead of decades, then let's enjoy the time, however short it might be.

Even temporary friendships create lasting memories. Remember the high school friend you walked home with almost every day? The girl you used to spend hours with, listening to tunes? We'd say goodbye, promise to keep in touch. For a time we would call, write, and visit. But years and distance took their toll, and well-meant promises too soon faded away.

Still we remember them. Still we are better people because of them. Let's not let the fear of parting tomorrow rob us of the time we have today.

Time is no measure for a sense of fulfillment. If we have today, let's make good use of it.

We will go our separate ways
better people because we traveled the same path for a mile or two.

We may never celebrate a "silver anniversary." But our friendship, for whatever time we have together, is golden.